Cakes for KIDS

Juliette Lalbaltry
Photography by **Delphine Constantini**

Cakes for KIDS

40 EASY RECIPES
THAT WILL WOW !

GIBBS SMITH
TO ENRICH AND INSPIRE HUMANKIND

Feel like
baking a cake?
**HERE'S HOW
TO DO IT!**

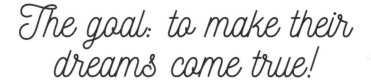

The goal: to make their dreams come true!

When it was suggested to me that I write my own book of cakes for kids, I immediately knew this project was right up my alley. For several weeks, I worked on creating cakes that were childlike, sweet, and full of wonder, taking into account the many interests of children and imagining their greatest dreams and fantasies. My ideas came together, and that's how I ended up with each one of these 40 fun creations.

What kid wouldn't dream of munching his or her very own pirate ship, nibbling a fruit-flavored goldfish, or devouring a bunch of flying saucers in space? Just imagine the smile of a boy or girl making Christmas sweets in the shape of a unicorn, and you'll understand clearly how every second spent putting this book together was a joy.

As a child, I discovered cooking by making cakes with my grandmother. I remember that I was a curious little girl, eager to taste every ingredient on the table and try out each and every stage of pastry-making.

Today, it's that same pleasure, that same love of pastries that I wish to share with you. I hope to encourage children to make the cakes of their dreams on their own (with a little help from an adult). I hope they will be happy and proud when they are finished decorating them, and of course, I want them to enjoy tasting their fabulous creations. All these recipes were designed to be as simple as possible—not a single stage is complicated, and still, the results are always amazing.

Start with one of four foolproof basic cakes (yogurt cake, chocolate cake, lemon cake, and vanilla sponge cake), choose the recipe you want to make, and put your creation together in just a few simple steps. I've marked the simplest recipes with READY, SET, BAKE, for days when everything's a bit of a rush, and the most ambitious recipes with WARNING: MASTERPIECE, for days when you have an extra 10 minutes or so to spare. That's right: even the most complicated recipes in this book are truly a piece of cake.

Now it's up to you. Play with these cake recipes and be sure to keep one goal in mind: have fun and enjoy!

JULIETTE LALBALTRY

P.S. Want a tip? The real secret to having fun with the cakes in this book is being creative with the decorating.

Table of Contents
FOR YOUNG CAKE-MAKERS

NOTE FOR PARENTS: **HERE ARE THE FOUR BASIC CAKES TO MASTER**

Bear Cubs
AT THE BEACH

The Race
TRACK

Circus
ANIMALS

The Candy
TRAIN

Polar
ICE FLOE

Tarzan's
JUNGLE

The Chocolate
CASTLE

The Flaky
CHRISTMAS TREE

Rosy-Cheeked
SANTA CLAUS

R-R-R
R-R-R

Lollipop
CHRISTMAS TREES

The Halloween
GRAVEYARD

King
CAKE POPS

The Great
EASTER EGG NEST

Rainbow
ROLL

Crunchy
CHOCOLATE NESTS

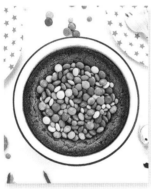

The Giant
M&M'S COOKIE

Chocolate and
BANANA CRÊPE SUSHI

The Rainbow
IN UNICORN LAND

The Birthday
PLANTER

Mother's Day
BOUQUET

The Flower Power
CAKE FOR GRANDMA

Yogurt CAKE

FOR **6 TO 8 KIDS** · PREPARATION: **10 MINUTES**
BAKING TIME: **40 MINUTES**

INGREDIENTS

—

¹/₂ cup plain yogurt
1 cup granulated sugar
1 teaspoon vanilla extract
4 eggs
2 cups all-purpose flour + more for the pan
1¹/₂ teaspoons baking powder
¹/₄ cup sunflower oil
Butter, for greasing the pan

—

1. Preheat the oven to 350°F. In a mixing bowl, whisk together the yogurt, sugar, vanilla, and eggs.

2. Sift the flour and baking powder together. Add to the wet ingredients and mix well to break up any lumps. Incorporate the oil.

3. Butter and flour an 8-inch round cake pan then pour the cake batter into the pan.

4. Bake for 40 minutes. Keep baking for a few minutes if the cake isn't done. Let the cake cool to room temperature before removing it from the pan.

Chocolate
CAKE

FOR **6 TO 8 KIDS** · PREPARATION: **10 MINUTES**
BAKING TIME: **35 MINUTES**

INGREDIENTS

—

7 ounces dark chocolate
$^1/_2$ cup unsalted butter + more for the pan
4 eggs
$^2/_3$ cup granulated sugar
$^3/_4$ cup all-purpose flour + more for the pan
$1^1/_2$ teaspoons baking powder
Pinch of salt

—

1. Preheat the oven to 350°F. Break the chocolate into pieces, cut the butter into cubes, then transfer both ingredients to a measuring cup. Melt in the microwave.

2. Separate the egg yolks and whites into two separate bowls.

3. Add the sugar to the egg yolks and beat until the mixture is light in color. Add the melted chocolate mixture then mix well to incorporate. Sift the flour and baking powder together then whisk into the wet ingredients.

4. Add the salt to the bowl with the egg whites and whisk until stiff peaks form. Gently fold the egg whites into the cake batter.

5. Butter and flour an 8-inch round cake pan then pour the cake batter into the pan.

6. Bake for 35 minutes. Keep baking for a few minutes if the cake isn't done. Let the cake cool to room temperature before removing it from the pan.

Lemon
CAKE

INGREDIENTS

—

1 cup all-purpose flour + more for the pan
1$\frac{1}{2}$ teaspoons baking powder
4 eggs
$\frac{2}{3}$ cup granulated sugar
$\frac{1}{3}$ cup unsalted butter + more for the pan
Juice from 3 lemons
Pinch of salt

—

1. Preheat the oven to 350°F. Sift the flour and baking powder together.

2. Divide the egg yolks and whites into two separate mixing bowls.

3. Add the sugar to the egg yolks and beat until the mixture is light in color.

4. Melt the butter in the microwave then add it to egg yolk mixture and whisk to combine.

5. Incorporate the lemon juice then the sifted flour and baking powder.

6. Add the salt to the bowl with the egg whites and whisk until stiff peaks form. Gently fold the egg whites into the cake batter.

7. Butter and flour an 8-inch cake pan then pour the cake batter into the pan.

8. Bake for 35 minutes. Keep baking for a few minutes if the cake isn't done. Let the cake cool to room temperature before removing it from the pan.

Rolled
SPONGE CAKE

FOR **6 TO 8 KIDS** · PREPARATION: **15 MINUTES**
BAKING TIME: **35 MINUTES**

INGREDIENTS

—

4 eggs
1 teaspoon vanilla extract
²/₃ cup granulated sugar
1 cup all-purpose flour

—

1. Preheat the oven to 350°F. Divide the egg yolks and whites into two mixing bowls. To the egg yolks, add the vanilla and sugar and beat until the mixture is light in color.

2. Whisk the egg whites until stiff peaks form. Add a small quantity of the whisked egg whites to the egg yolk mixture and whisk to incorporate. Gently fold in the remaining egg whites.

3. Sift the flour and add it to the egg mixture. Fold to fully incorporate then spread the batter over a parchment paper–lined baking sheet. Bake for 10 minutes. Keep baking for a few minutes if the cake isn't done.

4. Moisten a clean kitchen towel and spread it over a working surface. Flip the cake directly onto the towel.

5. Gently roll the cake into a log shape using the kitchen towel then let the cake cool to room temperature. This will allow the cake to remain soft and supple. Gently unroll the cake and remove the towel.

The Bunny
IN A SHIRT

FOR **6 TO 8 KIDS** · PREPARATION: **30 MINUTES**
BAKING TIME: **40 MINUTES**

INGREDIENTS

—

1 cup plain yogurt
2 cups granulated sugar
2 teaspoons vanilla extract
8 eggs
4 cups all-purpose flour
+ more for the pan
1 tablespoon baking powder
1/2 cup sunflower oil
Butter, for greasing the pan

—

TO DECORATE

—

2 toothpicks
1/2 cup chocolate-hazelnut spread
2 Lu Chocolate Barquettes or other oval-
shaped thumbprint cookies
2 star-shaped candies
1 large pink Haribo Dragibus or Dots
6 Mikado or Pocky cookies
7 small red Haribo Dragibus or Sixlets
1 small bag M&M's
3 small yellow candies
1 heart-shaped candy

—

1. Prepare 2 yogurt cakes following the instructions on p. 10, using the quantities listed above.

2. Cut out two arcs from one of the cakes to make the rabbit's ears. Use the rest of the cake to shape his body and head, pressing one cake into the other.

3. Place the ears on top of the head and stabilize them with toothpicks if needed.

4. Coat the whole cake with chocolate-hazelnut spread then smooth the surface with a rubber spatula.

5. Place 1 Lu Barquette over each ear. Use two star-shaped candies to make the eyes and make the pupils by adding two dabs of chocolate-hazelnut spread.

6. Place one large pink Dragibus candy on the head to make the nose, and six Mikado cookies for the whiskers, snapping off the part that isn't covered with chocolate.

7. Make a mouth using the small red Dragibus candies and decorate the rabbit's body with M&M's. Decorate the shirt with the heart-shaped candy and yellow candies.

The Rainbow
BUTTERFLY

FOR **6 TO 8 KIDS** · PREPARATION: **45 MINUTES**
BAKING TIME: **35 MINUTES**

INGREDIENTS

1 cup all-purpose flour
+ more for the pan
1¹/₂ teaspoons baking powder
4 eggs
²/₃ cup granulated sugar
¹/₃ cup unsalted butter
+ more for the pan
Juice from 3 lemons
Pinch of salt

—

TO DECORATE

¹/₃ cup chocolate-hazelnut spread
1 bag M&M's Minis (or regular)
Multicolored round sprinkles
9 marshmallow strawberries or
red gumdrops
2 Mikado or Pocky cookies

—

1. Prepare 1 lemon cake following the instructions on p. 12, using the quantities listed above.

2. Spread the whole cake with chocolate-hazelnut spread then smooth the surface with a rubber spatula.

3. Cut the cake into 4 pieces then arrange the wings as shown, leaving some space between the two sides. Leave some space between the top and bottom parts of the wings to make them bigger.

4. Decorate each wing with an outline made of M&M's then fill with sprinkles.

5. Create the body of the butterfly by lining up the marshmallow strawberries then stick 2 pieces of Mikado cookies (uncovered parts only) in the first gumdrop to make the antennae. Stick 2 blue M&M's Minis to the tips of the antennae using a bit of chocolate-hazelnut spread.

The Squinting
SPIDER

FOR **6 TO 8 KIDS** · PREPARATION: **30 MINUTES**
BAKING TIME: **35 MINUTES**

INGREDIENTS

7 ounces dark chocolate
1/2 cup unsalted butter
+ more for the pan
4 eggs
2/3 cup granulated sugar
3/4 cup all-purpose flour
+ more for the pan
1 1/2 teaspoons baking powder
Pinch of salt

TO DECORATE

1/2 cup chocolate-hazelnut spread
Chocolate sprinkles
1 large white marshmallow
2 small candy or plastic eyes
8 Cadbury Fingers

1. Prepare 1 chocolate cake and 2 cupcakes following the instructions on p. 11, using the quantities listed above. When it's time to pour the batter into the molds, fill 2 cupcake cups three-quarters of the way up then pour the remaining batter into the cake pan. Bake the cupcakes for 20 minutes and the cake for an additional 15 minutes, for a total of 35 minutes.

2. Place the cake on a large plate then add the 2 cupcakes at the top of the cake to make the eyes. Coat the cake and cupcakes with chocolate-hazelnut spread then smooth the surface with a rubber spatula.

3. Decorate the spider's entire body (but not its eyes) with chocolate sprinkles.

4. Cut 1 marshmallow into two rounds and stick 1 piece onto each cupcake to make the eyes. Add the 2 candy or plastic eyes. (If using plastic eyes, remove before eating.)

5. Place 4 Finger cookies on each side, between the cupcakes and the main cake, to create the spider's 8 legs.

The Busy BEES

FOR **6 TO 8 KIDS** · PREPARATION: **40 MINUTES**
BAKING TIME: **40 MINUTES**

INGREDIENTS

—

¹/₂ cup plain yogurt
1 cup granulated sugar
1 teaspoon vanilla extract
4 eggs
2 cups all-purpose flour
+ more for the pan
1¹/₂ teaspoons baking powder
¹/₄ cup sunflower oil
1 tablespoon butter, for greasing the pan

—

TO DECORATE

—

¹/₂ cup apricot jam
6 apricots halves in syrup
1 black pastry decorating pen
or icing tube
1 white pastry decorating pen
or icing tube
12 almond slices
7 raspberry candies
(Like Haribo or Jelly Belly)

—

1. Prepare 1 yogurt cake following the instructions on p. 10, using the quantities listed above.

2. Cover the cake with apricot jam then place 6 apricot halves, cut side down, on top.

3. Using the black pastry decorating pen, draw stripes over each apricot to create the bees' bodies. Add a full black circle at one end of each apricot to create their heads.

4. Use the white pastry decorating pen to draw the bees' eyes.

5. Stick 2 almond slices in each apricot half to make the wings.

6. Add the raspberry candies on top of the cake to mimic flowers.

Psychedelic
CATERPILLAR

FOR **10 KIDS** · PREPARATION: **1 HOUR**
BAKING TIME: **30 MINUTES**

INGREDIENTS

—

¹/₂ cup plain yogurt
1 cup granulated sugar
1 teaspoon vanilla extract
4 eggs
2 cups all-purpose flour
+ more for the pan
1¹/₂ teaspoons baking powder
¹/₄ cup sunflower oil

—

TO DECORATE

—

Yellow, red, and blue food coloring
²/₃ cup heavy cream
¹/₂ cup powdered sugar
2 purple Skittles or M&M's
1 bag Haribo Dragibus or Dots
1 (1-inch) piece of red candy thread
(thin licorice or Twizzlers Pull 'n' Peel)
1 black pastry decorating pen
or icing tube

—

1. Prepare 1 yogurt cake batter following the first two instructions on p. 10, using the quantities listed above. After step 2, divide the batter between 5 bowls then stir in food coloring to give each bowl of batter a different color: purple, green, yellow, red, and blue.

2. Line 10 muffin tin cups with paper liners then divide each color of batter between two cups to create 2 cupcakes in each color. Bake for 30 minutes then let cool.

3. Whip the cream and sugar together until the cream is stiff. Transfer to a pastry bag fitted with a star tip. Pipe some whipped cream on one cupcake then place a second cupcake sideways over the first to create the caterpillar's head. Add more whipped cream over the two assembled cupcakes then add 2 purple Skittles for the eyes, one red Dragibus candy for the nose, and the red candy thread for the mouth. Add two black dots on the eyes using the pastry decorating pen.

4. Pipe some whipped cream on each remaining cupcake and stick them sideways to one another to create the caterpillar's body. Use toothpicks to stick two blue Dragibus candies into the head to make antennae, and place plenty of Dragibus candies in different colors on both sides of the caterpillar's body to create the legs.

The Fruity
PEACOCK

FOR **6 TO 8 KIDS** · PREPARATION: **40 MINUTES**
BAKING TIME: **40 MINUTES** · RESTING TIME: **1 HOUR**

INGREDIENTS

—

¹/₂ cup plain yogurt
1 cup granulated sugar
1 teaspoon vanilla extract
4 eggs
2 cups all-purpose flour
1¹/₂ teaspoons baking powder
¹/₄ cup sunflower oil
Butter, for the pan

—

TO DECORATE

—

1 egg white
1¹/₄ cups powdered sugar
5 drops lemon juice
¹/₂ pear
1 carrot slice
1 white pastry decorating pen
1 black pastry decorating pen
9 green grapes
22 blueberries
9 raspberries
4 strawberries

—

1. Prepare 1 yogurt cake following the instructions on p. 10, using the quantities listed above.

2. Make the royal icing: whip the egg white, powdered sugar, and lemon juice together until smooth. Pour the icing over the top of the cake only then smooth it with a rubber spatula. Let the icing set for 1 hour at room temperature.

3. Place the pear half at the base of the cake. Cut out two tiny feet and one beak from the carrot slice then place them on the pear to complete the body.

4. Make two eyes by drawing two circles with the white pastry decorating pen (or an icing tube) then add 2 dots with the black pastry decorating pen, or use plastic or candy eyes.

5. Slice the grapes in halves and place them around the peacock's body to create the first arc of "feathers." Create a second row with blueberries, a third one with raspberries, a fourth with the remaining grape halves, then strawberry halves, and finally blueberries.

The Roaring
LION

FOR **6 TO 8 KIDS** · PREPARATION: **40 MINUTES**
BAKING TIME: **40 MINUTES**

INGREDIENTS

—

¹/₂ cup plain yogurt
1 cup granulated sugar
1 teaspoon vanilla extract
4 eggs
2 cups all-purpose flour
+ more for the pan
1¹/₂ teaspoons baking powder
¹/₄ cup sunflower oil
1 tablespoon butter, for greasing the pan

—

TO DECORATE

—

2 Oreo cookies
2 small candy or plastic eyes
1 black spiral licorice
1 bag of orange, yellow, and red square
or rectangular fruit jelly candies, or
sliced gumdrops

—

1. Prepare 1 yogurt cake following the instructions on p. 10, using the quantities listed above.

2. Split open two Oreos, taking care to leave all the cream on one of the two sides. Place the iced cookie halves over the cake to make the eyes. Top with candy or plastic eyes. (If using plastic eyes, remove before eating.)

3. Cut 1 of the leftover Oreo cookie sides in half then put one half under the eyes to create the nose. Unroll a spiral licorice then cut it into 6 equal pieces to make the whiskers. Place the whiskers on either side of the nose then set one orange jelly candy over the nose.

4. Cut two more strips of licorice to make the lion's mouth, starting from the nose and extending outwards.

5. Decorate the outer edge of the cake with jelly candies, alternating colors to create a beautiful mane.

The Cat
IN A SUIT

FOR **6 TO 8 KIDS** · PREPARATION: **50 MINUTES**
BAKING TIME: **35 MINUTES** RESTING TIME: **1 HOUR**

INGREDIENTS

—

4 eggs
1 cup all-purpose flour
2/3 cup granulated sugar
1/3 cup unsalted butter
+ more for the pan
1 1/2 teaspoons baking powder
Pinch of salt
Juice from 3 lemons

—

TO DECORATE

—

1 egg white + 1 1/4 cups powdered sugar
5 drops lemon juice
2 red sour belts or Fruit Roll-Ups
1 white marshmallow + 6 Cadbury Fingers
1 bag small Haribo Dragibus or Sixlets
1 chocolate pastry decorating pen
1 bag large Haribo Dragibus or Dots
1 pink M&M's Mini
1 Lu Chocolate Barquette
or other oval-shaped
thumbprint cookie

—

1. Prepare 1 lemon cake following the instructions on p. 12, using the quantities listed above.

2. Make the royal icing: whip the egg white, powdered sugar, and lemon juice together until smooth.

3. Pour the icing over the cake then smooth it with a spatula. Let set for 1 hour at room temperature.

4. Make a bow tie using sour belts: unroll a long strip and fold the ends of towards the center. Cut a narrow strip out of a second piece and wrap around the folded strip to hold the bow tie together. Place under the cat's head.

5. Cut one marshmallow into 2 rounds and place them on the cake to create the eyes. Top with two small blue Dragibus candies then draw the eyes and eyebrows using the pastry decorating pen.

6. Place two large pink Dragibus candies and one small pink Dragibus in an inverted triangle below the eyes to make the cat's nose then add 1 pink M&M's Mini in the center of the triangle. Draw the cat's mouth using the pastry decorating pen.

7. Place 3 Fingers on each side of the nose to make the whiskers.

8. Cut the Lu Barquette into two pieces and set them at the top of the cake to make the ears.

The Cute
OWL

FOR **6 TO 8 KIDS** · PREPARATION: **35 MINUTES**
BAKING TIME: **35 MINUTES**

INGREDIENTS

7 ounces dark chocolate
1/2 cup unsalted butter
+ more for the pan
4 eggs
2/3 cup granulated sugar
3/4 cup all-purpose flour
+ more for the pan
1 1/2 teaspoons baking powder
Pinch of salt

TO DECORATE

1/3 cup chocolate-hazelnut spread
About 20 cat's tongue cookies or other
oval cookies, like Milano or Vienna Fingers
Multicolored round sprinkles
2 Oreo cookies
2 small pink Haribo Dragibus or Sixlets
1 small red candy
6 red square or rectangular
fruit jelly candies,
or sliced gumdrops

1. Prepare 1 chocolate cake following the instructions on p. 11, using the quantities listed above.

2. Cut out an arc from the top of the cake and discard to create the top of the owl's body. Coat the whole cake with chocolate-hazelnut spread then smooth the surface with a rubber spatula.

3. Make the feathers: layer the cat's tongue cookies on either side of the cake, leaving an empty triangle in the middle. Fill the triangle with sprinkles.

4. Split open two Oreos, taking care to leave all the cream on one of the two sides. Place the iced cookie halves on the cake to make the eyes. Top with 2 small pink Dragibus or Dots candies to finish the eyes then add one small red candy to make the beak.

5. Place 3 fruit jellies in a triangle shape over one of the points at the top of the cake to create an ear then repeat to make the second ear. Fill up each ear with sprinkles.

The Goldfish
IN A BOWL

FOR **6 TO 8 KIDS** · PREPARATION: **40 MINUTES**

BAKING TIME: **40 MINUTES**

INGREDIENTS

—

¹/₂ cup plain yogurt

1 cup granulated sugar

1 teaspoon vanilla extract

4 eggs

2 cups all-purpose flour
+ more for the pan

1¹/₂ teaspoons baking powder

¹/₄ cup sunflower oil

1 tablespoon butter, for greasing the pan

—

TO DECORATE

—

8 ounces whipped cream cheese

2 tablespoons granulated sugar

12 marshmallow strawberries or red gumdrops

1 bag red and pink M&M's Minis, M&M's, or Sixlets (Specialty colors can be found online.)

1 pint fresh strawberries

—

1. Prepare 1 yogurt cake following the instructions on p. 10, using the quantities listed above.

2. Cut a 2-inch wide triangular-shaped piece from the cake (like you were cutting a small piece to serve) and place it on the other side of the cake, rounded side away from the cake, to make the tail.

3. Mix the cream cheese with the sugar then cover the cake completely with this mixture. Smooth with a rubber spatula.

4. Outline the head of the goldfish with red and pink M&M's Minis. Use 1 marshmallow strawberry for the eye.

5. Wash and trim the strawberries then cut them into slices. Place them on the body of the fish, all going the same way, to create the scales. Add pink M&M's Minis between each one of them then cover the entire tail with marshmallow strawberries.

Lemon Island
TURTLES

FOR **6 TO 8 KIDS** · PREPARATION: **30 MINUTES**
BAKING TIME: **35 MINUTES** · RESTING TIME: **1 HOUR**

INGREDIENTS

1 cup all-purpose flour
+ more for the pan

1^1/$_2$ teaspoons baking powder

4 eggs

^{2}/$_3$ cup granulated sugar

^{1}/$_3$ cup unsalted butter
+ more for the pan

Juice from 3 lemons

Pinch of salt

TO DECORATE

1 egg white

1^1/$_4$ cups powdered sugar

5 drops lemon juice

1 kiwi

13 grapes

10 black sesame seeds, or 1 chocolate
decorating pen or icing tube

5 marshmallow strawberries
or red gumdrops

5 large green Haribo Dragibus or Dots

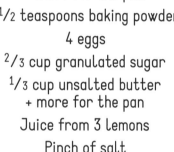

1. Prepare 1 lemon cake following the instructions on p. 12, using the quantities listed above.

2. Make the royal icing: whip the egg white, powdered sugar, and lemon juice together until smooth. Add more powdered sugar if the icing looks too thin, or a few drops of lemon juice if it looks too thick.

3. Pour the icing over the surface of the cake, leaving ^{1}/$_4$ inch clear around the edge, and smooth it with a rubber spatula. Let the icing set for 1 hour at room temperature.

4. Peel the kiwi then cut it into thick slices. Place the kiwi slices on the cake, spacing them apart.

5. Cut 3 grapes in half to make the turtles' heads and place at the end of each kiwi slice then add 2 black sesame seeds for the eyes (or draw 2 dots of chocolate with a pastry decorating pen).

6. Cut off the ends of the other grapes then place them around each kiwi slice to create 4 legs on each turtle.

7. Place 1 marshmallow strawberry on each turtle's back then scatter the large green Dragibus candies on the cake.

Snails
HAVING A PICNIC

FOR **6 SNAILS** · PREPARATION: **35 MINUTES**
BAKING TIME: **25 MINUTES** · RESTING TIME: **30 MINUTES**

INGREDIENTS

4 eggs
1 teaspoon vanilla extract
$^2/_3$ cup granulated sugar
1 cup all-purpose flour

TO DECORATE

$^2/_3$ cup chocolate-hazelnut spread
1 bag M&M's Minis
1 bag small Haribo Dragibus or Dots
30 toothpicks
1 black pastry decorating pen
Marshmallow strawberries or
red gumdrops
Marshmallow bananas or banana-shaped
Runts candies

1. Prepare 1 rolled sponge cake following the instructions on p. 13, using the quantities listed above.

2. Place the sponge cake on a baking sheet and spread it generously with chocolate-hazelnut spread. Roll it up, leaving the final 1¼ inch unrolled to make the snails' heads. Refrigerate the snails for 30 minutes.

3. Cut off the ends of the rolled sponge in order to have neat edges. Cut the rolled sponge into 6 slices, each about 1¼-inch-wide, to form the snails.

4. Decorate the snails' heads with 2 colors of M&M's Minis, changing colors from one snail to the next. Stick 2 small identical Dragibus candies on the ends of two wooden toothpicks to make the antennae and stick them on the head of a snail. Repeat for all the snails. If desired, add 2 black dots on each eye using a black pastry decorating pen.

5. Press 2 small Dragibus candies into the middle of the sponge rolls, on either side of the snails. Decorate the shell of 3 of the snails with marshmallow strawberries and the other 3 with marshmallow bananas, using toothpick pieces (or frosting, if using Runts) to hold them in place.

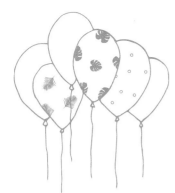

Hungry
WOLF

FOR **6 TO 8 KIDS** · PREPARATION: **45 MINUTES**
BAKING TIME: **35 MINUTES**

INGREDIENTS

7 ounces dark chocolate
$^1/_2$ cup unsalted butter
+ more for the pan
4 eggs
$^2/_3$ cup granulated sugar
$^3/_4$ cup all-purpose flour
+ more for the pan
$1^1/_2$ teaspoons baking powder
Pinch of salt

—

TO DECORATE

$^1/_3$ cup chocolate-hazelnut spread
2 chocolate Lu Barquettes or other oval-
shaped thumbprint cookies
4 large white marshmallows
2 small candy or plastic eyes
1 red sour belt or Fruit Roll-Ups
1 large black Haribo Dragibus or Dots
6 Mikado or Pocky cookies

—

1. Prepare 1 chocolate cake in a loaf pan following the instructions on p. 11, using the quantities listed above.

2. Spread the entire cake with chocolate-hazelnut spread then smooth the surface with a rubber spatula.

3. Place 2 chocolate Lu Barquettes on the back of the cake to form the two ears.

4. Lay two marshmallows sideways on the top of the cake to make the eyes then add 2 small plastic or candy eyes, sticking them in place with a dot of chocolate-hazelnut spread. (If using plastic eyes, remove before eating.)

5. Make a 3-inch-deep cut opposite the ears, starting from the front. Cut 2 marshmallows in little triangles to create the teeth then place them in the sliced opening.

6. Add a strip of sour belt for the tongue and place one large black Dragibus candy on top of the cake to make the nose.

7. Stick 6 Mikado cookies on either side of the wolf's snout for the whiskers.

Blue-Eyed
SHEEP

FOR **6 TO 8 KIDS** · PREPARATION: **30 MINUTES**
BAKING TIME: **35 MINUTES**

INGREDIENTS

1 cup all-purpose flour
+ more for the pan

1 1/2 teaspoons baking powder

4 eggs

2/3 cup granulated sugar

1/3 cup unsalted butter
+ more for the pan

Juice from 3 lemons

Pinch of salt

TO DECORATE

8 ounces whipped cream cheese

3 tablespoons granulated sugar

1 bag large white marshmallows

2 large pink marshmallows

2 blue candies

1 small black Haribo Dragibus or Sixlet

1 chocolate pastry decorating pen or
icing tube

Pink round sprinkles

1. Prepare 1 lemon cake following the instructions on p. 12, using the quantities listed above.

2. Whisk the whipped cream cheese with the sugar then cover the whole cake with the frosting. Smooth the surface with a rubber spatula.

3. Place 2 rows of white marshmallows standing up all around the edge of the cake, and swap in 2 pink marshmallows towards the top of the head to make the lamb's ears. Add two more rows of marshmallows (as shown in the photo) to finish off the head.

4. Add 2 blue candies to the part that has been left uncovered to make the eyes then draw two dots using the chocolate pastry decorating pen to create the pupils.

5. Place the small black Dragibus candy for the nose then draw the mouth using the pastry decorating pen.

6. Spread a little more of the cream cheese mixture on the ears and decorate with pink sprinkles.

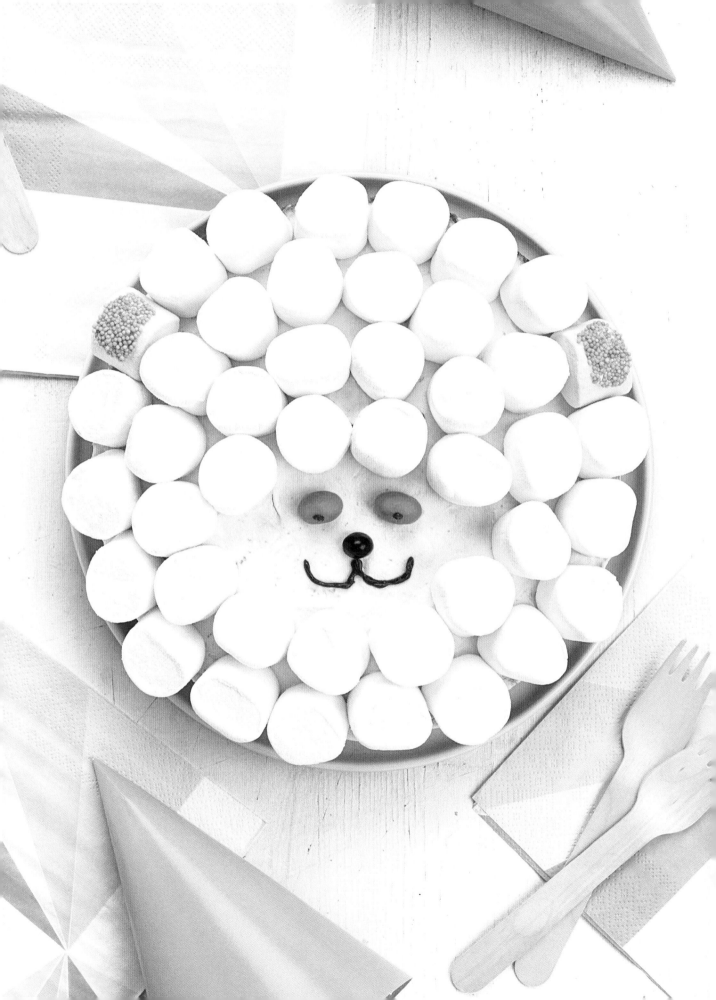

The Adorable
HEDGEHOG

FOR **6 TO 8 KIDS** • PREPARATION: **40 MINUTES**
BAKING TIME: **40 MINUTES**

INGREDIENTS

7 ounces dark chocolate
$^{1}/_{2}$ cup unsalted butter
+ more for the pan
4 eggs
$^{2}/_{3}$ cup granulated sugar
$^{3}/_{4}$ cup all-purpose flour
+ more for the pan
$1^{1}/_{2}$ teaspoons baking powder
Pinch of salt

TO DECORATE

$^{1}/_{3}$ cup chocolate-hazelnut spread
2 large black Haribo Dragibus or Dots
1 small pink candy
1 black spiral licorice or Twizzlers
Pull 'n' Peel
1 box of Mikado or Pocky cookies

1. Prepare 1 chocolate cake following the instructions on p. 11, using the quantities listed above.

2. Cut off and discard two small triangles from the bottom of the cake to create the hedgehog's head. Spread the entire cake with chocolate-hazelnut spread then smooth the surface with a rubber spatula.

3. Place 2 large black Dragibus candies to create the eyes and 1 small pink candy for the nose.

4. Cut off 6 1-inch licorice pieces and place 3 pieces on each side of the head to create the whiskers.

5. Cut each Mikado cookie in thirds and place them all over the cake to create the spikes. The more there are, the better it will look!

Clown
FACES

FOR **6 TO 8 KIDS** · PREPARATION: **45 MINUTES**
BAKING TIME: **35 MINUTES**

INGREDIENTS
—

14 ounces dark chocolate
1 cup unsalted butter
+ more for the pan
8 eggs
1¹⁄₃ cups granulated sugar
1¹⁄₂ cups flour + more for the pans
1 tablespoon baking powder
2 pinches of salt

TO DECORATE
—

²⁄₃ cup chocolate-hazelnut spread
5 waffle ice cream cones
1 bag large Haribo Dragibus or Dots
25 marshmallow strawberries
or red gumdrops
1 bag M&M's Minis
Chocolate pastry decorating pen
5 small red Haribo
Dragibus or Sixlets
1 red or multicolored
Twizzlers Pull 'n' Peel
—

1. Prepare 2 chocolate cakes following the instructions on p. 11, using the quantities listed above.

2. Place the first cake on a serving plate and spread the surface with chocolate-hazelnut spread. Put the second cake on top of the first then cover the top and sides of the layered cake with more chocolate-hazelnut spread.

3. Cut the ice cream cones so that they are all the same height, also making sure they stand straight once inverted. Place them on top of the cake, evenly spaced around the edge.

4. Decorate the space around the cones by forming circles with large Dragibus candies of various colors then add 1 marshmallow strawberry between each cone.

5. Place 2 M&M's Minis of the same color under each of the cones, on the side of the cake, to make the clowns' eyes. Add black dots using a pastry decorating pen for the pupils and place 1 small red Dragibus candy under each set of eyes to create the noses.

6. Cut off 1-inch pieces from a strand of Twizzlers and stick them under the noses to create the mouths. Decorate the entire bottom of the cake with marshmallow strawberries.

The Polar
BEAR

FOR **6 TO 8 KIDS** · PREPARATION: **40 MINUTES**
BAKING TIME: **40 MINUTES**

INGREDIENTS

—

¹/₂ cup plain yogurt
1 cup granulated sugar
1 teaspoon vanilla extract
4 eggs
2 cups all-purpose flour
+ more for the pan
1¹/₂ teaspoons baking powder
¹/₄ cup sunflower oil
Butter, for greasing the pan

—

TO DECORATE

—

8 ounces whipped cream cheese
3 tablespoons granulated sugar
3 cups sweetened shredded coconut
3 Oreos
2 small candy or plastic eyes
1 spiral black licorice or Twizzlers
Pull 'n' Peel
2 Pépito Mini-Rollos or
thumbprint cookies

—

1. Prepare 1 yogurt cake following the instructions on p. 10, using the quantities listed above.

2. Whisk the whipped cream cheese with the sugar then spread it all over the cake. Generously sprinkle with coconut.

3. Split open two Oreos, taking care to leave all the cream on one of the two sides. Place the iced cookie halves on the cake to make the bear's eyes. Top with 2 small candy or plastic eyes. (If using plastic eyes, remove before eating.)

4. Cut 1 Oreo in half and place 1 half under the eyes to create the nose.

5. Cut off 3 1-inch pieces of black licorice and use them to make the eyebrows and the top of the mouth then cut off a final 2-inch piece to draw the bear a nice smile.

6. Finally, place 2 thumbprint cookies on the top of the cake to create the bear's ears.

The Pirate
SHIP

FOR **6 TO 8 KIDS** · PREPARATION: **1 HOUR**
BAKING TIME: **35 MINUTES**

INGREDIENTS

7 ounces dark chocolate
1/2 cup unsalted butter
+ more for the pan
4 eggs
2/3 cup granulated sugar
3/4 cup all-purpose flour
+ more for the pan
1 1/2 teaspoons baking powder
Pinch of salt

TO DECORATE

1/2 cup chocolate-hazelnut spread
1 box Mikado or Pocky cookies
1 bag M&M's or M&M's Minis
2 chocolate-filled wafers
11 small red candies
6 rolled wafer cookies (such as Pirouette)
1 star-shaped candy
Large gold sprinkles
1 red sour belt or Fruit Roll-Ups
1 tube of edible glue

1. Prepare 1 chocolate cake in a loaf pan following the instructions on p. 11, using the quantities listed above.

2. Cut the front of the cake in a point then cut a 1-inch slice off from the back part and set aside.

3. Cover the cake with chocolate-hazelnut spread. Place the 1-inch slice over the flat rear part of the cake and cover it with chocolate-hazelnut spread as well.

4. Make the railing using Mikado cookies: insert 2 cookies on the back corners of the cake then attach another piece of cookie horizontally above them on each side of the ship using chocolate-hazelnut spread. Add two diagonal railings on the front of the ship. Decorate the sides of the ship with M&M's.

5. Place 1 chocolate-filled wafer vertically toward the back of the ship then balance a second wafer over the cake slice and the edge of the first wafer to create the cabin.

6. Decorate the front and back of the cake with small red candies.

7. Place 3 rolled wafers on each side of the ship to make cannons and add a star-shaped candy to the prow. Decorate the bridge with a mound of golden sprinkles and make a flag with 1 Mikado cookie, 1 piece of sour belt candy, and some edible glue (or caramel).

Flying Saucers
IN SPACE

FOR **6 TO 8 KIDS** · PREPARATION: **30 MINUTES**
BAKING TIME: **35 MINUTES**

INGREDIENTS

—

7 ounces dark chocolate

1/2 cup unsalted butter
+ more for the pan

4 eggs

2/3 cup granulated sugar

3/4 cup all-purpose flour
+ more for the pan

1 1/2 teaspoons baking powder

Pinch of salt

—

TO DECORATE

—

1/2 egg white

2/3 cup powdered sugar

2 drops lemon juice

Small white and yellow candy stars or
star-shaped sprinkles

20 wooden skewers

1 box of flying saucer candies or satellite
or Nilla Wafers (about 20, available
online)

—

1. Prepare 1 chocolate cake following the instructions on p. 11, using the quantities listed above.

2. Make the royal icing: whip the egg white, powdered sugar, and lemon juice together until smooth. Add some powdered sugar if the icing looks too thin, or a few drops of lemon juice if it looks too thick.

3. Pour the icing into a pastry bag fitted with a fine round tip. Draw a spiral over the entire cake, starting at the center.

4. Sprinkle the entire surface with candy stars.

5. Cut the wooden skewers to various lengths and stick one end of each skewer into a flying saucer candy or Nilla Wafer cookie (you may need to glue the cookies on with frosting or caramel) and the other end into the cake in different spots.

Bear Cubs
AT THE BEACH

FOR **6 TO 8 KIDS** • PREPARATION: **40 MINUTES**
BAKING TIME: **35 MINUTES**

INGREDIENTS

7 ounces dark chocolate

$^1/_2$ cup unsalted butter
+ more for the pan

4 eggs

$^2/_3$ cup granulated sugar

$^3/_4$ cup all-purpose flour
+ more for the pan

$1^1/_2$ teaspoons baking powder

Pinch of salt

TO DECORATE

4 shortbread cookies

4 green sour belts or Fruit Roll-Ups

5 wooden skewers

3 rolled wafer cookies

1 red sour belt or Fruit Roll-Ups

1 bag gummy bears

1 orange Fruit Roll-Up, or sour belt candy

2 chocolate Lu Barquettes or other oval-
shaped thumbprint cookies

1. Prepare 1 chocolate cake following the instructions on p. 11, using the quantities listed above.

2. Using a food processor or a mortar and pestle, crush the shortbread cookies to a coarse powder. Spread the powder over $^3/_4$ of the top of the cake to create the beach.

3. Cut out leaves of various sizes from the green sour belts and stick them onto 3 of the wooden skewers to create the palm tree leaves. Insert the skewers into rolled wafer cookies and stick the "trees" into the beach side of the cake.

4. Cut out small rectangles from the red sour belt to make tiny beach towels. Place them on the cookie beach then lay gummy bears over the towels.

5. Cut out 2 small rectangles from the orange sour belt. Attach 1 piece on each Lu Barquette with a wooden skewer to create 2 little sailboats. Add the bears as sailors and put them on the water side of the cake.

The Race
TRACK

FOR **6 TO 8 KIDS** · PREPARATION: **30 MINUTES**
BAKING TIME: **35 MINUTES**

INGREDIENTS

7 ounces dark chocolate
1/2 cup unsalted butter
+ more for the pan
4 eggs
2/3 cup granulated sugar
3/4 cup all-purpose flour
+ more for the pan
1 1/2 teaspoons baking powder
Pinch of salt

—

TO DECORATE

1 sheet paper
Powdered sugar
1 small bag M&M's
6 Oreos
1 straw

—

1. Prepare 1 chocolate cake following the instructions on p. 11, using the quantities listed above.

2. Draw a road design on a sheet of paper, including the road striping. Carefully cut out the design to make a stencil, and place the stencil on the cake. Pour the powdered sugar into a fine sieve then sprinkle the entire cake without moving the paper. Very carefully remove the stencil.

3. Outline the road with M&M's and place a small car on it.

4. Place a pile of Oreos on one side of the road a second smaller pile on the other side to look like piles of tires.

5. To make the finish line, print a rectangular black and white checkerboard and attach it with adhesive tape across 2 halves of a cut straw. Insert the straws into the cake on each side of the road and that's all there is to it!

Circus
ANIMALS

FOR **6 TO 8 KIDS** · PREPARATION: **40 MINUTES**
BAKING TIME: **40 MINUTES**

INGREDIENTS

¹/₂ cup plain yogurt
1 cup granulated sugar
1 teaspoon vanilla extract
4 eggs
2 cups all-purpose flour
+ more for the pan
1¹/₂ teaspoons baking powder
¹/₄ cup sunflower oil
Butter, for greasing the pan

—

TO DECORATE

²/₃ cup chocolate-hazelnut spread
1 bag small Haribo Dragibus or Sixlets
3 shortbread cookies
1 box Mikado or Pocky cookies
25 marshmallow strawberries or
red gumdrops

—

1. Prepare 1 yogurt cake following the instructions on p. 10, using the quantities listed above.

2. Spread the top of the cake with chocolate-hazelnut spread then smooth the surface with a rubber spatula.

3. Outline a circle of about 4 inches in diameter in the center of the cake using small Dragibus candies of various colors.

4. Using a food processor or a mortar and pestle, crush the shortbread cookies to a coarse powder. Fill the Dragibus circle with this cookie powder.

5. Stick Mikado cookies between the Dragibus candies and the cookie powder to create vertical bars.

6. Place marshmallow strawberries all around the edge of the cake.

7. Add a few circus animal figurines on and around the cake.

The Candy
TRAIN

FOR **6 TO 8 KIDS** · PREPARATION: **50 MINUTES**
BAKING TIME: **35 MINUTES**

INGREDIENTS

—

7 ounces dark chocolate
1/2 cup unsalted butter
+ more for the pan
4 eggs
2/3 cup granulated sugar
3/4 cup all-purpose flour
+ more for the pan
1 1/2 teaspoons baking powder
Pinch of salt

—

TO DECORATE

—

1/2 cup chocolate-hazelnut spread
10 Pépito Mini-Rollos or
thumbprint cookies
1 bag M&M's
1 rectangular shortbread cookie
(such as Petit Beurre)
1 box Mikado or Pocky cookies
Large pink marshmallows

—

1. Prepare 1 chocolate cake in a loaf pan following the instructions on p. 11, using the quantities listed above.

2. Cut the cake crosswise into 3 equal parts. Cut a slice about 1 inch thick from the first piece of cake then place the slice on top of the cut piece of cake to form the cabin of the locomotive. Spread the three cars all over with chocolate-hazelnut spread.

3. Attach 2 thumbprint cookies on either side of the locomotive, and 4 more on each of the two cars to make the wheels.

4. Decorate the front of the train with M&M's of various colors and set the shortbread cookie on top of the locomotive to create a roof.

5. Stick Mikado cookies into the tops of the two cars around the edges to create cages then fill them with pink marshmallows. Strengthen the cages with colored string to make the train even more beautiful!

QUICK AND EASY **READY, SET, BAKE!** A PIECE OF CAKE!

Polar
ICE FLOE

FOR **6 TO 8 KIDS** · PREPARATION: **40 MINUTES**
BAKING TIME: **40 MINUTES**

INGREDIENTS

—

$^1/_2$ cup plain yogurt
1 cup granulated sugar
1 teaspoon vanilla extract
4 eggs
2 cups all-purpose flour
+ more for the pan
$1^1/_2$ teaspoons baking powder
$^1/_4$ cup sunflower oil
Butter, for greasing the pan

—

TO DECORATE

—

8 ounces whipped cream cheese
3 tablespoons granulated sugar
3 cups sweetened shredded coconut
1 bag large white marshmallows
1 bag small blue Haribo Dragibus or
Sixlets (or similar small, round candies)

—

1. Prepare 1 yogurt cake following the instructions on p. 10, using the quantities listed above.
2. Whisk the whipped cream cheese with the sugar then spread it all over the cake.
3. Smooth the surface with a rubber spatula then generously sprinkle the cake with coconut.
4. Make a little ice mountain using marshmallows then draw a river using blue Dragibus candies.
5. Place a few polar animal figurines on the cake and add marshmallows all around.

Tarzan's
JUNGLE

FOR **6 TO 8 KIDS** · PREPARATION: **50 MINUTES**
BAKING TIME: **35 MINUTES**

INGREDIENTS

—

7 ounces dark chocolate
$\frac{1}{2}$ cup unsalted butter
+ more for the pan
4 eggs
$\frac{2}{3}$ cup granulated sugar
$\frac{3}{4}$ cup all-purpose flour
+ more for the pan
$1\frac{1}{2}$ teaspoons baking powder
Pinch of salt

—

TO DECORATE

—

1 egg white
$1\frac{1}{4}$ cups powdered sugar
5 drops lemon juice
A few drops green food coloring
4 green sour belts or Fruit Roll-Ups
2 packages rolled wafer cookies
3 wooden skewers
1 box Mikado or Pocky cookies
6 marshmallow bananas or banana Runts
1 bag Skittles

—

1. Prepare 1 chocolate cake following the instructions on p. 11, using the quantities listed above.

2. Make the royal icing: whip the egg white, sugar, lemon juice, and food coloring together until smooth. Add more powdered sugar if the icing looks too thin, or a few drops of lemon juice if it looks too thick.

3. Cover the entire surface of the cake with the royal icing and smooth with a rubber spatula.

4. Place rolled wafer cookies all around the cake then tie a string around the cake. If using taller cookies, like Pirouette wafers, break into halves or thirds to match the height of the cake.

5. Cut out leaves from the sour belt and stick them onto the wooden skewers to create the palm tree leaves. Insert the skewers into the wafer cookies and distribute them over the cake.

6. Break some Mikado cookies in half then stick them in various places over the cake.

7. Add some marshmallow bananas and Skittles to represent fallen fruits.

8. Decorate with small monkey figurines on the cake and in the trees.

The Chocolate
CASTLE

FOR **6 TO 8 KIDS** • PREPARATION: **1 HOUR**

BAKING TIME: **35 MINUTES**

INGREDIENTS

7 ounces dark chocolate
1/2 cup unsalted butter
+ more for the pan
4 eggs
2/3 cup granulated sugar
3/4 cup all-purpose flour
+ more for the pan
1 1/2 teaspoons baking powder
Pinch of salt

TO DECORATE

1/2 cup chocolate-hazelnut spread
20 Lu Prince or other vanilla
sandwich cookies
1 package Cadbury Fingers
1 Lu Chocolate Barquette or other oval-
shaped thumbprint cookie
4 waffle ice cream cones
6 marshmallow strawberries or
red gumdrops
1 bag M&M's Minis
1 white pastry decorating pen or icing
tube

1. Prepare 1 chocolate cake following the instructions on p. 11, using the quantities listed above.

2. Cut out 4 semicircles the same size as half of a sandwich cookie from the 4 "corners" of the cake.

3. Spread the whole cake with chocolate-hazelnut spread then smooth the surface with a rubber spatula.

4. Make 4 towers out of 5 sandwich cookies by placing a dab of chocolate-hazelnut spread between each cookie to hold them together. Place the towers where you cut out the holes in the cake.

5. Cover the side of the cake with Finger cookies, leaving a space about 1 inch wide on one of the sides. Set 1/2 of a chocolate Lu Barquette into that spot to create the door.

6. Cut off the top of the ice cream cones so that they are flat then place one over each of the towers to form the tops. Stick 1 marshmallow strawberry or gumdrop on each point.

7. Add 1 marshmallow strawberry in the center of the cake and one over the door.

8. Place M&M's all around the towers, attaching them with drops of icing from the pastry decorating pen.

The Flaky
CHRISTMAS TREE

FOR **6 TO 8 KIDS** · PREPARATION: **30 MINUTES**

QUICK AND EASY
**READY,
SET, BAKE!**
A PIECE OF CAKE !

INGREDIENTS

—

2 sheets puff pastry
1/2 cup chocolate-hazelnut spread
1 egg yolk

—

TO DECORATE

—

1 bag Skittles
1 bag small Haribo Dragibus or Sixlets
1 star-shaped candy

—

1. Preheat the oven to 350°F. Spread out both sheets of puff pastry on a work surface and cut them in the shape of identical Christmas trees.

2. Transfer one of the trees onto a baking sheet covered with parchment paper then spread all over with chocolate-hazelnut spread. Cover it with the second tree, being careful to align the edges.

3. Very delicately and without cutting through the pastry, trace two lines, from the base of the trunk up to the top of the tree.

4. Using a knife, slice branches about 1/3-inch thick on each side of the tree, leaving the center trunk uncut.

5. Holding both layers together, twist the branches back on themselves, all in the same direction.

6. Use a pastry brush to brush the entire tree with egg yolk. Bake for 25 minutes.

7. Let the tree cool then transfer it to a serving plate. Decorate the tree with Skittles and small Dragibus candies then add a star-shaped candy at the top.

Rosy-Cheeked
SANTA CLAUS

FOR **6 TO 8 KIDS** · PREPARATION: **40 MINUTES**

BAKING TIME: **40 MINUTES**

INGREDIENTS

¹/₂ cup plain yogurt

1 cup granulated sugar

1 teaspoon vanilla extract

4 eggs

2 cups all-purpose flour
+ more for the pan

1¹/₂ teaspoons baking powder

¹/₄ cup sunflower oil

Butter, for greasing the pan

TO DECORATE

³/₄ cup heavy cream

¹/₃ cup powdered sugar

About 45 marshmallow strawberries or
red gumdrops

1 large white marshmallow

2 small black Haribo Dragibus or Sixlets

1 small pink Haribo Dragibus or Sixlets

2 small candy or plastic eyes

1 large pink marshmallow

1. Prepare 1 yogurt cake following the instructions on p. 10, using the quantities listed above.

2. Make the whipped cream: add the heavy cream and sugar to the bowl of a stand mixer or a mixing bowl and whip until stiff peaks form. Transfer the whipped cream to a pastry bag fitted with a star tip. Pipe the whipped cream over the bottom of the cake, stopping half-way up the cake, to create Santa's beard and hair, leaving some space in the center of the cake for the face.

3. Cover the top half of the cake with marshmallow strawberries to represent Santa Claus' hat, using dabs of the whipped cream for glue. Use 3 marshmallow strawberries to make the point of the hat over one side of Santa's face, and the white marshmallow at the tip to create the pompom (as shown in the photo).

4. Add 2 small black Dragibus candies for the eyes and top them with 2 small candy or plastic eyes. (If using plastic eyes, remove before eating.)

5. Place 1 small pink Dragibus for the nose and cut 1 pink Marshmallow in half for the cheeks.

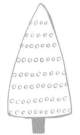

Lollipop
CHRISTMAS TREES

FOR **8 KIDS** · PREPARATION: **40 MINUTES**

BAKING TIME: **30 MINUTES** · RESTING TIME: **1 HOUR**

INGREDIENTS

—

7 ounces dark chocolate

1/2 cup unsalted butter
+ more for the pan

4 eggs

2/3 cup granulated sugar

3/4 cup all-purpose flour
+ more for the pan

1 1/2 teaspoons baking powder

Pinch of salt

—

TO DECORATE

—

1/2 cup chocolate-hazelnut spread

8 Popsicle sticks

1/2 egg white

2/3 cup powdered sugar

3 drops lemon juice

A few drops green food coloring

1 bag Skittles

1 bag M&M's Minis

—

1. Prepare 1 chocolate cake following the instructions on p. 11, using the quantities listed above.

2. Spread the whole cake with chocolate-hazelnut spread then smooth the surface with a rubber spatula. Slice the cake into 8 equal pieces then insert Popsicle sticks into the rounded end of each piece. Refrigerate for 30 minutes.

3. Make the royal icing: whip the egg white, powdered sugar, lemon juice, and food coloring together until smooth. Add more powdered sugar if the icing looks too thin, or a few drops of lemon juice if it looks too thick.

4. Pour the icing into a pastry bag fitted with a small round tip then draw garlands over each lollipop tree.

5. Use Skittles and M&M's Minis to decorate the trees then let them set at room temperature for 30 minutes.

The Halloween
GRAVEYARD

FOR **6 TO 8 KIDS** · PREPARATION: **40 MINUTES**

INGREDIENTS

7 ounces dark chocolate

$1/2$ cup unsalted butter
+ more for the pan

4 eggs

$2/3$ cup granulated sugar

$3/4$ cup all-purpose flour
+ more for the pan

$1 1/2$ teaspoons baking powder

Pinch of salt

TO DECORATE

$1/3$ cup chocolate-hazelnut spread

$1/2$ egg white

$2/3$ cup powdered sugar

5 drops lemon juice

3 cat's tongue cookies or other oval
cookies, like Milano or Vienna Fingers

1 chocolate pastry decorating pen

3 Oreos

1 package Mikado or Pocky cookies

2 yellow candy strings (licorice or
Twizzlers Pull 'n' Peel)

1. Prepare 1 chocolate cake following the instructions on p. 11, using the quantities listed above.

2. Spread the top of the cake with chocolate-hazelnut spread then smooth using a rubber spatula.

3. Make the royal icing: whip the egg white, powdered sugar, and lemon juice together until smooth.

4. Pour the icing into a pastry bag fitted with a small round tip then draw a spider web on one side of the cake: draw 7 lines about 2 inches long starting from the same point then add connecting arcs between each line. Let dry for about 30 minutes at room temperature.

5. With the pastry decorating pen (or icing tube), write "RIP" on the cat's tongue cookies then stick them vertically in the cake to make tombstones.

6. Open the Oreos, remove the frosting, then crumble the cookies. Sprinkle the crumbs in front of each tombstone to form small graves.

7. Stick several Mikado cookies into the cake and then make the brooms: cut off 16 1-inch strips from the candy strings then attach them to 2 Mikado cookies using a bit of string. Lay the brooms on the cake.

King
CAKE POPS

FOR **6 KIDS** · PREPARATION: **40 MINUTES**
BAKING TIME: **15 TO 20 MINUTES**

INGREDIENTS

½ cup unsalted butter,
room temperature
½ cup granulated sugar
1 cup ground almonds
2 eggs + 3 egg yolks, divided
2 sheets puff pastry

TO DECORATE

1 dried bean (or 6)
6 wooden skewers
Gold glitter paper

1. Preheat the oven to 350°F.

2. Make the frangipane: beat the butter and sugar together until creamy. Add the ground almonds, the eggs, and 2 egg yolks, and beat to incorporate. Set aside.

3. Spread out the sheets of puff pastry on a work surface then use a round cookie cutter or a glass to cut 6 rounds out of each sheet. Place 6 pastry rounds on a baking sheet lined with parchment paper then prick them with a fork.

4. Place a good amount of frangipane in the center of each disc, making sure to keep ½ inch clean around the edges. Brush the edges with egg yolk, slip 1 bean into 1 of the cake pops (or 1 in each cake pop), then cover every cake pop with a second round of puff pastry.

5. Press the edges together then roll them gently towards the center of the cookie to seal. Draw cute designs over each cake pop using a wooden skewer or a toothpick, without pushing too hard to avoid poking a hole through the pastry.

6. Brush the cake pops with egg yolk and bake 15 to 20 minutes. Let cool for a few minutes then stick a wooden skewer in each cake pop.

7. Cut little crowns out of glitter paper and place them over the cake pops.

8. The kid who finds the bean in their cake pop is King or Queen for the day. Or, if you used six beans, every kid gets to be King!

The Great
EASTER EGG NEST

FOR **6 TO 8 KIDS** · PREPARATION: **40 MINUTES**
BAKING TIME: **35 MINUTES** · RESTING TIME: **1 HOUR**

INGREDIENTS

7 ounces dark chocolate
¹/₂ cup unsalted butter
+ more for the pan
4 eggs
²/₃ cup granulated sugar
³/₄ cup all-purpose flour
+ more for the pan
1¹/₂ teaspoons baking powder
Pinch of salt

TO DECORATE

1 egg white
1¹/₄ cups powdered sugar
5 drops lemon juice
Multicolored round sprinkles
1 bag mini chocolate eggs

1. Prepare 1 chocolate cake in a Bundt pan following the instructions on p. 11, using the quantities listed above.

2. Make the royal icing: whip the egg white, powdered sugar, and lemon juice together until smooth. Add more powdered sugar if the icing looks too thin, or a few drops of lemon juice if it looks too thick.

3. Pour the icing over the top of the cake, letting it drip down the sides, but without covering it completely.

4. Add the sprinkles right away so they stick to the icing. Let the icing set for 1 hour at room temperature.

5. Transfer the cake to a serving plate and fill the center of the cake with chocolate eggs.

Rainbow
ROLL

FOR **6 TO 8 KIDS** · PREPARATION: **1 HOUR**

BAKING TIME: **35 MINUTES**

INGREDIENTS

4 eggs
1 teaspoon vanilla extract
2/3 cup granulated sugar
1 cup all-purpose flour
Food coloring

TO DECORATE

3/4 cup very cold heavy cream
1/3 cup powdered sugar
5 large Haribo Dragibus or
Dots candies in different colors

1. Prepare sponge cake batter following the first steps of recipe on p. 13. After incorporating the flour in step 3, divide the cake batter into 6 small bowls. Mix a few drops of food coloring into each bowl to obtain 6 different colors: red, orange, yellow, green, blue, and purple.

2. Transfer each batch of colored batter to a different pastry bag then pipe the first one in a long strip over a silicon baking sheet. Pipe all colors side-by-side. Bake for 10 minutes.

3. Moisten a clean kitchen towel and spread it on a work surface. Flip the cake directly onto the towel. Gently roll the cake along with the kitchen towel then let the cake cool to room temperature so it remains soft and supple.

4. Make the whipped cream: add the heavy cream and sugar to the bowl of a stand mixer or a mixing bowl, and whip until stiff peaks form.

5. Unroll the sponge cake, remove the towel, then spread the whipped cream all over the cake. Very gently roll up the cake again, removing any excess whipped cream with a rubber spatula.

6. Transfer the cake to a serving plate. Pipe 5 small rounds of whipped cream over the cake then top with 5 large Dragibus candies of various colors.

Crunchy
CHOCOLATE NESTS

FOR **12 NESTS** · PREPARATION: **30 MINUTES**
BAKING TIME: **5 MINUTES** · RESTING TIME: **1 HOUR**

INGREDIENTS

7 ounces baker's chocolate
$1/3$ cup unsalted butter, cubed
$1/3$ cup granulated sugar
8 cups unsweetened cornflakes

TO DECORATE

12 cupcake liners
1 bag M&M's Minis

1. Break the chocolate into pieces and melt it with the butter in the microwave.

2. Mix in the sugar then transfer to a large mixing bowl. Add the corn flakes. Mix well to fully coat the cornflakes with the melted chocolate mixture.

3. Place the cupcake liners in a cupcake pan then distribute the chocolate-cornflake mixture between the cups. Use a small spoon to press the mixture down the sides of the cups to create nests. Refrigerate for 1 hour.

4. Before serving, transfer the nests with their cupcake liners onto a serving plate then fill each nest with M&M's Minis.

The Giant
M&M'S COOKIE

FOR **6 TO 8 KIDS** · PREPARATION: **30 MINUTES**
BAKING TIME: **25 MINUTES**

INGREDIENTS

—

¹/₂ cup unsalted butter,
room temperature + more for the pan

²/₃ cup brown sugar

1 egg

1 teaspoon vanilla extract

³/₄ cup all-purpose flour

1 teaspoon baking powder

3¹/₂ ounces chocolate chips

¹/₂ teaspoon salt

—

TO DECORATE

—

1 bag M&M's
1 bag M&M's Minis

—

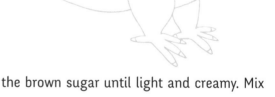

1. Preheat the oven to 350°F. Beat the butter with the brown sugar until light and creamy. Mix in the egg and vanilla.

2. Sift the flour and baking powder together then add to the batter. Mix well with a spatula then incorporate the chocolate chips and salt. Butter an 8-inch round cake pan. Spread the batter into the pan then bake for 20 minutes.

3. Let cool for 10 minutes then add the M&M's and M&M's Minis to the center of the cookie. Serve warm with a big glass of milk for a real treat.

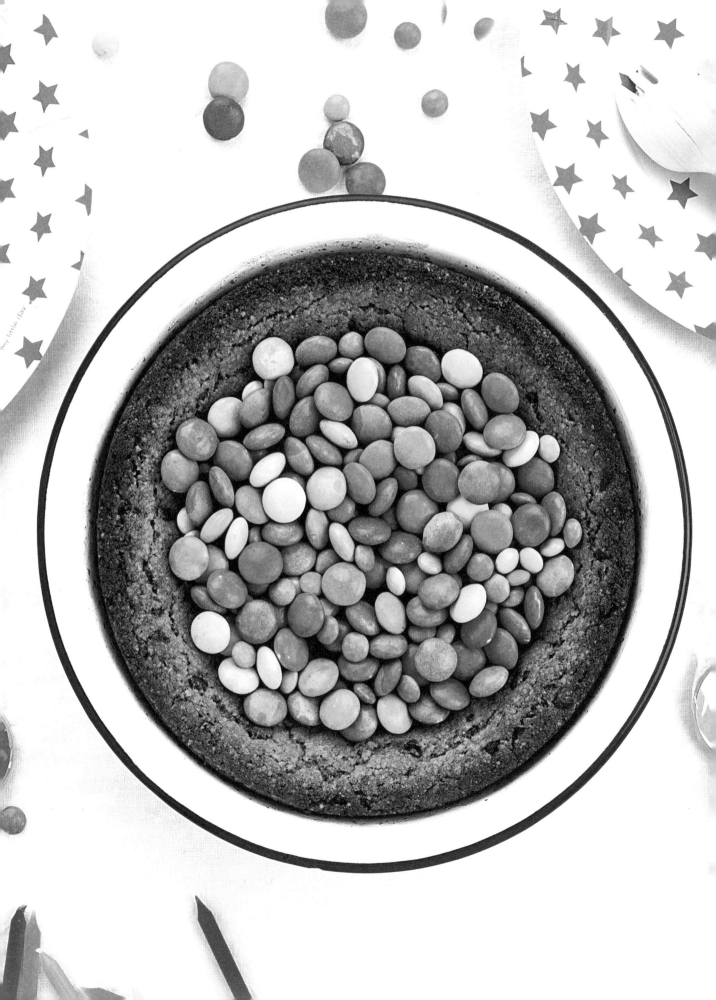

Chocolate and
BANANA CRÊPE SUSHI

FOR **6 TO 8 KIDS** · PREPARATION: **30 MINUTES**
COOKING TIME: **15 MINUTES**
RESTING TIME: **1 HOUR**

INGREDIENTS

—

3/4 cup all-purpose flour
3 eggs
1 teaspoon vanilla extract
Pinch of salt
1 tablespoon hot chocolate powder
2 cups milk
3 tablespoons unsalted butter
+ more for cooking

—

TO DECORATE

—

1/2 cup chocolate-hazelnut spread
3 bananas
1 package mixed candies
Decorative toothpicks

—

1. In a large mixing bowl, combine the flour, eggs, vanilla, salt, and hot chocolate powder. Slowly mix in the milk, whisking to avoid lumps.

2. Melt the butter in the microwave then add it to the mixture. Let the batter rest for 1 hour at room temperature.

3. Melt a small amount of butter in a skillet then pour in a ladle of the crêpe batter. Swirl the skillet to distribute the batter evenly then cook the crêpe for about 1 minute. Flip it over and cook for 1 minute more. Transfer the crêpe to a plate. Repeat to cook all the crêpes.

4. Spread each crêpe with chocolate-hazelnut spread then roll them up around halved bananas. Cut the edges neatly to make pretty little sushi rolls and stick a candy on each one using a decorative toothpick.

The Rainbow
IN UNICORN LAND

FOR **6 TO 8 KIDS** · PREPARATION: **40 MINUTES**
BAKING TIME: **35 MINUTES**

INGREDIENTS

7 ounces dark chocolate
1/2 cup unsalted butter
+ more for the pan
4 eggs
2/3 cup granulated sugar
3/4 cup all-purpose flour
+ more for the pan
1 1/2 teaspoons baking powder
Pinch of salt

TO DECORATE

1/3 cup chocolate-hazelnut spread
2 bags M&M's
1 package small white marshmallows

1. Prepare 1 chocolate cake following the instructions on p. 11, using the quantities listed above.

2. Spread the whole cake with chocolate-hazelnut spread then smooth the surface with a rubber spatula.

3. Make the top row of the rainbow by creating a circular arc around the top half of the cake using blue M&M's.

4. Follow up with green, yellow, orange, and red M&M's closing in to the center of the cake.

5. Create 2 big clouds by making mounds of marshmallows. Enjoy, but don't forget to invite the unicorn!

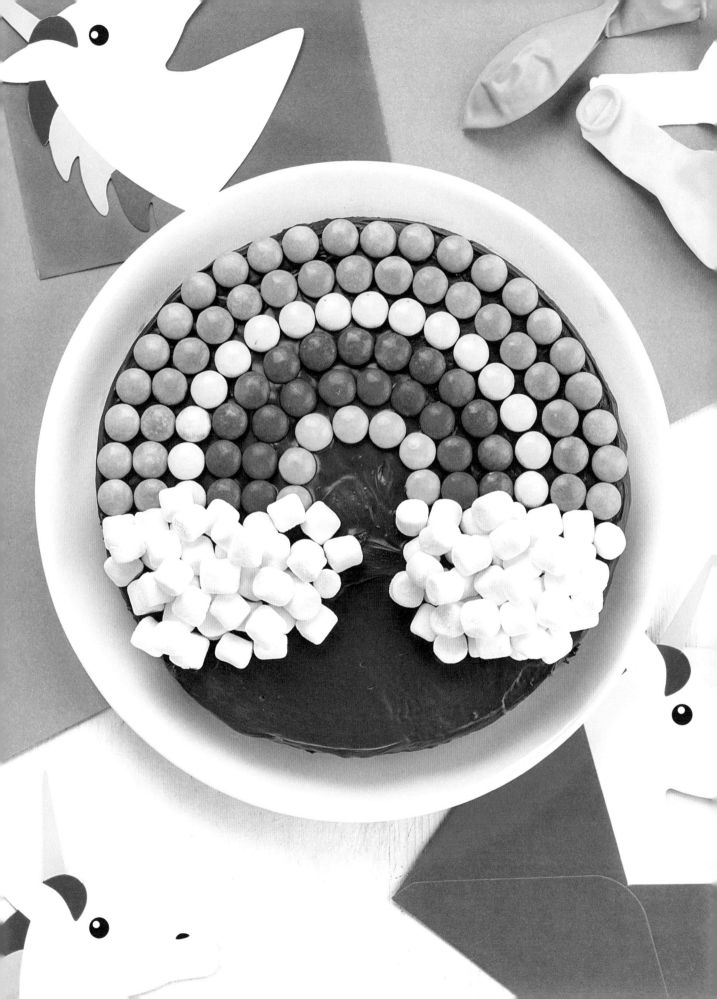

The Birthday
PLANTER

FOR **6 TO 8 KIDS** · PREPARATION: **45 MINUTES**

BAKING TIME: **35 MINUTES**

INGREDIENTS

7 ounces dark chocolate

$1/2$ cup unsalted butter
+ more for the pan

4 eggs

$2/3$ cup granulated sugar

$3/4$ cup all-purpose flour
+ more for the pan

$1 1/2$ teaspoons baking powder

Pinch of salt

TO DECORATE

$1/3$ cup chocolate-hazelnut spread

About 20 cat's tongue cookies or other
oval cookies, like Milano or Vienna Fingers

5 Oreos

10 Mikado or Pocky cookies

5 green sour belts or Fruit Roll-Ups

10 marshmallow strawberries or
red gumdrops

10 flower-shaped candies

10 berry-shaped candies (like Jelly Belly)

5 large Haribo Dragibus or Dots

1. Prepare 1 chocolate cake in a loaf pan following the instructions on p. 11, using the quantities listed above.

2. Cover the entire cake with chocolate-hazelnut spread then line up cat's tongue cookies vertically around the sides. Tie a piece of string around the cookies to support, and to make a cute decoration.

3. Discard the white frosting from the Oreos then crumble the cookies and spread them in the planter box to make the soil.

4. Create flowers by sticking various candies on Mikado cookies then create leaves by cutting them out of green sour belts. Decorate the cake with the flowers and leaves then enjoy!

Mother's Day
BOUQUET

FOR **1 BOUQUET** · PREPARATION: **30 MINUTES**

INGREDIENTS

—

1 bag large Haribo Dragibus or Dots candies
1 bag large white marshmallows
1 bag marshmallow strawberries or red gumdrops
1 bag marshmallow bananas
4 green sour belts or Fruit Roll-Ups
Toothpicks
Wooden skewers

—

1. Begin by making flowers out of Dragibus candies: stick 1 large Dragibus, flat surface toward the top, onto a skewer, then slide 1 marshmallow strawberry onto the skewer, and top with another Dragibus. Poke a toothpick through the marshmallow strawberry and stick 1 Dragibus on each side of the toothpick. Repeat to make 6 petals.

2. Follow the same instructions to create all the flowers using different colors then repeating to make flowers out of the marshmallow bananas.

3. Make the marshmallow flowers: fold the edges of a sour belt towards the center then stick them on skewers. Stick 1 white marshmallow on top and end with 1 marshmallow strawberry.

The Flower Power
CAKE FOR GRANDMA

FOR **6 TO 8 KIDS** · PREPARATION: **45 MINUTES**
BAKING TIME: **35 MINUTES**

INGREDIENTS

—

7 ounces dark chocolate

1/2 cup unsalted butter
+ more for the pan

4 eggs

2/3 cup granulated sugar

3/4 cup all-purpose flour
+ more for the pan

1 1/2 teaspoons baking powder

Pinch of salt

—

TO DECORATE

—

1 1/2 cups chocolate-hazelnut spread

About 20 cat's tongue cookies or other
oval cookies, like Milano or Vienna Fingers

1 bag M&M's

1 bag M&M's Minis

Round sprinkles

—

1. Prepare 1 chocolate cake following the instructions on p. 11, using the quantities listed above.

2. Spread the whole cake with chocolate-hazelnut spread then smooth the surface with a rubber spatula.

3. Line up cat's tongue cookies vertically all around the cake (the cookies will stick to the chocolate-hazelnut spread) then tie a pretty string around the cake.

4. Make several flowers of various sizes and colors using mini and regular M&M's.

5. Decorate the cake with sprinkles.

Index of ingredients

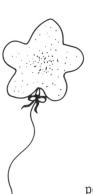

Author's Acknowledgments

A big thank you to Émilie and Marion for assigning me this very pretty project and especially for having confidence in me!

A huge thank you to one of my favorite brands, "My Little Day," which loaned us all the party accessories, disposable tableware, decorations, straws, napkins, etc. They are the perfect partner for organizing a party—for adults as well as children! Thank you to the entire team for their kindness and availability.

Website: www.mylittleday.fr

Thank you to Maxime and the entire team at Green Alternative for their support and compliments—and for eating the majority of the cakes!

First Edition

23 22 21 20 19   5 4 3 2 1

Published in the United States of America by
Gibbs Smith
P.O. Box 667
Layton, Utah 84041
1.800.835.4993 orders
www.gibbs-smith.com

Text © 2019 Juliette Lalbaltry
Photographs © 2019 Delphine Constantini
Illustrations: Shutterstock © Goosefrol

ISBN 13: 978-1-4236-5282-3
Library of Congress Control Number: 2019936913

First published in France as *Gâteaux Kids: 40 Recettes Ultra-Simples Pour Un Effet Wahou!*
©Larousse 2018
21 Rue du Montparnasse
75006 Paris, France

Publication directors: Isabelle Jeuge-Maynart and Ghislaine Stora
Editorial director: Émilie Franc
Editors: Marion Dellapina and Alice Delbarre
Cover designer: Valentine Antenni
Interior designer: Émilie Laudrin
Proofreader: Maud Foutieau
Production: Donia Faiz and Marine Garguy